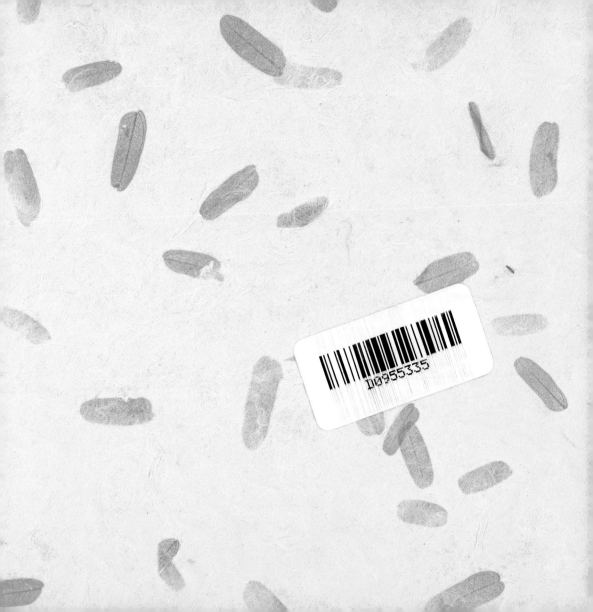

Dearest Muriel,

Those who have lived in our hearts
are never really gone.
As long as we keep them with us,
in our hearts and our thoughts,
they will be with us always.
For love, which is timeless,
never ceases to exist.

S. E. MacNaughton

We love you and wish you
well with prayers & thoughts.

Rick & Linda Davidson

The *"Language of"* Series...

Words of
COMFORT
...for You in Your Time of Loss

A Blue Mountain Arts® Collection

Blue Mountain Press ™

SPS Studios, Inc., Boulder, Colorado

Library of Congress Catalog Card Number: 2001005882
ISBN: 0-88396-625-5

We wish to thank Susan Polis Schutz for permission to reprint the following poem that appears in this publication: "The loss of a person is felt deeply by many...." Copyright © 2002 by Susan Polis Schutz.

ACKNOWLEDGMENTS appear on page 48.

Certain trademarks are used under license.

Manufactured in Thailand
First Printing: January 2002

 This book is printed on recycled paper.

Library of Congress Cataloging-in-Publication Data

Words of comfort : —for you in your time of loss.
      p. cm. — ("Language of— " series)
"A Blue Mountain Arts collection"—P.
  ISBN 0-88396-625-5 (hardcover : alk. paper)
  1.   Consolation—Quotations, maxims, etc.   I. SPS Studios. II. Series.
  PN6084.C57 W59 2002
  291.4'42—dc21

                                                                    2001005882
                                                                         CIP

SPS Studios, Inc.
P.O. Box 4549, Boulder, Colorado 80306

Contents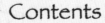

(Authors listed in order of first appearance)

A Message of
Comfort and Consolation

A loved one is a treasure of the heart, and losing a loved one is like losing a piece of yourself. But the love that this person brought you did not leave, for the essence of the soul lingers. It cannot escape your heart, for it has been there forever.

Cling to the memories and let them find their way to heal you. The love and laughter, the joy in the togetherness you shared, will make you strong. You'll come to realize that your time together, no matter how long, was meant to be and that you were blessed to have such a precious gift of love in your life.

Keep your heart beating with the loving memories, and trust in your faith to guide you through. Know that, though life moves on, the beauty of love stays behind to surround and embrace you. Your loved one has left you that... to hold in your heart forever.

 debbie peddle

To Everything, There Is a Season…

A time of love, a time of sharing,
and a time of memories.
In each season,
let yesterday's memories lead you.
In every time of need,
count the blessings, not the tears.
Fill your heart with the best of the past,
and hope will come to you.

Keep your eyes on the good times,
and feel the love surrounding you.
There will always be times of trial,
but for every sorrow, there is hope;
for every tear, there is love.
As you work your way through
this time of sadness,
may strong and lasting memories
be your comfort.
As you journey down this road
of many branching paths…
let's walk together.

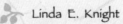
Linda E. Knight

When somebody dies, a cloud turns into an angel and flies up to tell God to put another flower on a pillow. A bird gives the message back to the world and sings a silent prayer that makes the rain cry. People disappear, but they never really go away. The spirits up there put the sun to bed, wake up the grass, and spin the Earth in dizzy circles. Sometimes you can see them dancing in a cloud during the daytime when they're supposed to be sleeping. They paint the rainbows and also the sunsets and make waves splash and tug at the tide. They toss shooting stars and listen to wishes. And when they sing windsongs, they whisper to us, "Don't miss me too much. The view is nice, and I'm doing just fine."

 Ashley Rice

Death Is a Door

Death is only an old door
Set in a garden wall;
On gentle hinges it gives, at dusk
When the thrushes call.

Along the lintel are green leaves,
Beyond the light lies still;
Very willing and weary feet
Go over that sill.

There is nothing to trouble any heart;
Nothing to hurt at all.
Death is only a quiet door
In an old wall.

Nancy Byrd Turner

The life of man seems to me like the flight of a sparrow through the hall wherein you are sitting at supper in the winter time, a warm fire lighted on the hearth while storms rage without. The sparrow flies in at one door, tarries for a moment in the light and heat, and then flying forth through another door vanishes into the wintry darkness whence it had come. So tarries man for a brief space, but of what went before or what is to follow, we know not.

The Venerable Bede

Ships Returning Home

We all are ships returning home laden with life's experience, memories of work, good times and sorrows, each with his special cargo;

And it is our common lot to show the marks of the voyage, here a shattered prow, there a patched rigging, and every hulk turned black by the unceasing batter of the restless wave.

May we be thankful for fair weather and smooth seas, and in times of storm have the courage and patience that mark every good mariner;

And, over all, may we have the cheering hope of joyful meetings, as our ship at last drops anchor in the still water of the eternal harbor.

Max Ehrmann

It seemeth such a little way to me,
Across to that strange country, the Beyond;
And yet, not strange, for it has grown to be
The home of those of whom I am so fond;
They make it seem familiar and most dear,
As journeying friends bring distant countries near.

And so for me there is no sting to death,
And so the grave has lost its victory;
It is but crossing with abated breath
And white, set face, a little strip of sea,
To find the loved ones waiting on the shore,
More beautiful, more precious than before.

Ella Wheeler Wilcox

Immortality

It cannot be that earth is man's only abiding place. It cannot be that our life is a bubble, cast up by the ocean of eternity, to float another moment upon its surface, and then sink into nothingness and darkness forever. Else why is it that the high and glorious aspirations which leap like angels from the temples of our hearts, are forever wandering abroad, satisfied?

Why is it that the rainbow and the cloud come over us with a beauty that is not of earth, and then pass off and leave us to muse on their faded loveliness?...

Finally, why is it that bright forms of human beauty are presented to the view, and then taken from us, leaving the thousand streams of the affections to flow back in an Alpine torrent upon our hearts?

We are born for a higher destiny than that of earth. There is a realm where the rainbow never fades; where the stars will be spread out before us like the islands that slumber on the ocean; and where the beautiful beings that here pass before us like visions will stay in our presence forever!

George D. Prentice

There Is No Death

There is a plan far greater than the plan you know;
There is a landscape broader than the one you see.
There is a haven where storm-tossed souls may go —
You call it death — we, immortality.
You call it death — this seeming endless sleep;
We call it birth — the soul at last set free.
'Tis hampered not by time or space — you weep.
Why weep at death? 'Tis immortality.

Farewell, dear voyager — 'twill not be long.
Your work is done — now may peace rest with thee.
Your kindly thoughts and deeds — they will live on.
This is not death — 'tis immortality.

Farewell, dear voyager — the river winds and turns;
The cadence of your song wafts near to me,
And now you know the thing that all men learn:
There is no death — there's immortality.

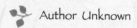 Author Unknown

The Loss of a Loved One Is Never Easy

The loss of a loved one leaves a big space in the heart that may take a while to heal; we feel that part of us is gone. Sorrow makes us feel unsteady and lonely. The resolutions of any problems or unaccepted solutions are now up to us to work out with ourselves in our hearts and minds. There may be things we wish we had said or done or hadn't done that will make this transition more complicated and painful for us. Tears help, but sometimes it seems they bring no relief because we can't change what has happened.

Grief is a very personal and individual process that needs to run its course. We each need to respond to it in our very own way. There are no wrongs or rights, but we shouldn't bury our hurt alive. Sometimes it helps to talk about it. Sometimes it helps to apply any increased awareness gleaned from this experience to others in our lives and become more conscious of ways to love them and to show our love better.

When we lose someone we love, we go through changes that we don't understand as we adjust to the loss. We may become overly sensitive and not know why; we may pull away from those we love because we know deep down that we could lose them, too, and we just can't stand the thought of dealing with that kind of hurt again right now.

During this time, we may go through different stages and degrees of withdrawal. We may want to sleep more or we may not be able to sleep much. We may want to eat more — or less. We may cry more easily. We may become more withdrawn, or we may not want to be alone at all. We may avoid allowing close relationships to develop for a while, or we may draw closer to someone we don't seem to have anything in common with.

The loss of a loved one is never easy, but as you move through this grief process, allow yourself to be comforted by others, knowing that you are in their thoughts and prayers.

 Donna Fargo

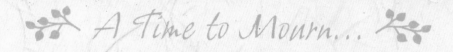

No one can tell you about grief, about its limitless boundaries, its unfathomable depths. No one can tell you about the crater that is created in the center of your body, the one that nothing can fill. No matter how many times you hear the word *final*, it means nothing until final is actually final.

 Ruth Coughlin

For us there is only one season, the season of sorrow. The very sun and moon seem taken from us.... it is always twilight in one's heart. And in the sphere of thought, no less than in the sphere of time, motion is no more. The thing that you personally have long ago forgotten, or can easily forget, is happening to me now, and it will happen to me again tomorrow.

 Oscar Wilde

Everyone can master a grief but he that hath it.

 William Shakespeare

Give sorrow words.... The grief that does not speak,
whispers the o'erfraught heart, and bids it break.

 William Shakespeare

Grief knits two hearts in closer bonds than happiness ever can,
and common suffering is a far stronger link than common joy.

 Alphonse de Lamartine

To One in Sorrow

Let me come in where you are weeping, friend,
And let me take your hand.
I, who have known a sorrow such as yours,
Can understand.
Let me come in — I would be very still
Beside you in your grief;
I would not bid you cease your weeping, friend,
Tears bring relief.
Let me come in — I would only breathe a prayer,
And hold your hand,
For I have known a sorrow such as yours,
And understand.

 Grace Noll Crowell

Sometimes, when one person is missing, the whole world seems depopulated.

Alphonse de Lamartine

The Bustle in a House

The bustle in a house
The morning after death
Is solemnest of industries
Enacted upon earth, —

The sweeping up the heart,
And putting love away
We shall not want to use again
Until eternity.

Emily Dickinson

I didn't plan to be this person, for whom loss always hovers at the edge of my awareness like next month's bills, but there you have it. I've carried the remote ache of longing with me long enough to understand it's part of who I am now.... This is a part of my identity that I can never change.... Our lives are shaped as much by those who leave us as they are by those who stay. Loss is our legacy. Insight is our gift. Memory is our guide.

Hope Edelman

We understand death for the first time when
he puts his hand upon one whom we love.

 Madame de Stael

The Rainy Day

The day is cold and dark and dreary;
It rains, and the wind is never weary;
The vine still clings to the moldering wall,
But at every gust the dead leaves fall,
   And the day is dark and dreary.

My life is cold and dark and dreary;
It rains, and the wind is never weary;
My thoughts still cling to the moldering past,
But the hopes of youth fall thick in the blast,
   And the days are dark and dreary.

Be still, sad heart! and cease repining;
Behind the clouds is the sun still shining:
Thy fate is the common fate of all:
Into each life some rain must fall,
   Some days must be dark and dreary.

 Henry Wadsworth Longfellow

The Comfort of Memories

There's a prayer that says the only way any of us ever achieve immortality is by living on in the hearts of those who love us and the thoughts of those who remember us.

Dr. Joy Browne

There is a remembrance of the dead, to which we turn even from the charms of the living. These we would not exchange for the song of pleasure or the bursts of revelry.

Washington Irving

Memory is more than a looking back to a time that is no longer; it is a looking out into another kind of time altogether where everything that ever was continues not just to be, but to grow and change with the life that is in it still. The people we loved. The people who loved us. The people who, for good or ill, taught us things.

Frederick Buechner

The life of the dead is placed in the memory of the living.

 Marcus Tullius Cicero

Memory

I have a room whereinto no one enters
   Save I myself alone:
   There sits a blessed memory on a throne,
There my life centres.

While winter comes and goes — oh tedious comer! —
   And while its nip-wind blows;
   While bloom the bloodless lily and warm rose
Of lavish summer.

If any should force entrance he might see there
   One buried yet not dead,
   Before whose face I no more bow my head
Or bend my knee there;

But often in my worn life's autumn weather
   I watch there with clear eyes,
   And think how it will be in Paradise
When we're together.

 Christina Rossetti

Comfort Is...

...knowing that those
who have lived in our hearts
are never really gone.
As long as we keep them with us,
in our hearts and our thoughts,
they will be with us always.

S. E. MacNaughton

...a deep gratefulness for having known and shared
in the life of a very special person.

D. H. Rogers

...like a door to the heart that can only be unlocked from the inside.

Gregory Walton

...a promise that no sorrow lasts forever; that consolation
resembles the rays of the sun or the ocean's waves, and it
surrounds you with understanding, compassion, and solace.

Edward Earl Brown

❧ *Consolation Is...* ❧

...like a seed that lies planted in the soul. It cannot and it will not bloom in the winter of the heart's grief, for winter is not its season. Instead, it lies dormant — for years, sometimes — until sorrow washes away, bright and clear, and leaves a space for consolation to grow. In that moment, it draws from the long roots it has been growing in the heart and blossoms forth in clusters of beautiful memories.

❧ Jordan St. Cyr

...the great gift that is yours to share with another soul in sorrow. It can be expressed best not in words, but simply by your silent presence and your willingness to stand beside this person as they seek a way through the vast and personal labyrinth of mourning.

❧ Lawrence B. Tavernas

...a little like a journey that each man must find his own map to navigate by.

❧ Jon Ericksson

You would know the secret of death.

But how shall you find it unless you seek it in the heart of life?

The owl whose night-bound eyes are blind unto the day cannot unveil the mystery of light.

If you would indeed behold the spirit of death, open your heart wide unto the body of life.

For life and death are one, even as the river and the sea are one.

In the depth of your hopes and desires lies your silent knowledge of the beyond;

And like seeds dreaming beneath the snow your heart dreams of spring.

Trust the dreams, for in them is hidden the gate to eternity.

Your fear of death is but the trembling of the shepherd when he stands before the king whose hand is to be laid upon him in honour.

Is the shepherd not joyful beneath his trembling, that he shall wear the mark of the king?

Yet is he not more mindful of his trembling?

For what is it to die but to stand naked in the wind and to melt into the sun?

And what is it to cease breathing, but to free the breath from its restless tides, that it may rise and expand and seek God unencumbered?

Only when you drink from the river of silence shall you indeed sing.

And when you have reached the mountain top, then you shall begin to climb.

And when the earth shall claim your limbs, then shall you truly dance.

Kahlil Gibran

Departed Friends

The dead friends live and always will;
Their presence hovers round us still.
It seems to me they come to share
Each joy or sorrow that we bear.
Among the living I can feel
The sweet departed spirits steal,
And whether it be weal or woe,
I walk with those I used to know.
I can recall them to my side
Whenever I am struggle-tried;
I've but to wish for them, and they
Come trooping gayly down the way,
And I can tell to them my grief
And from their presence find relief.
In sacred memories below
Still live the friends of long ago.

Edgar A. Guest

To Those I Love

If I should ever leave you whom I love
To go along the Silent Way, grieve not.
Nor speak of me with tears, but laugh and talk
Of me as if I were beside you there.
(I'd come — I'd come, could I but find a way!
But would not tears and grief be barriers?)
And when you hear a song or see a bird
I loved, please do not let the thought of me
Be sad... For I am loving you just as
I always have... You were so good to me!
There are so many things I wanted still
To do — so many things to say to you...
Remember that I did not fear... It was
Just leaving you that was so hard to face...
We cannot see Beyond... But this I know:
I loved you so — 'twas heaven here with you!

Isla Paschal Richardson

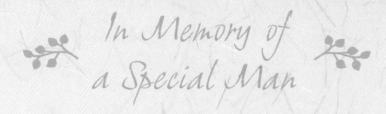

In Memory of a Special Man

Stop all the clocks, cut off the telephone,
Prevent the dog from barking with a juicy bone,
Silence the pianos and with muffled drum
Bring out the coffin, let the mourners come.

Let aeroplanes circle moaning overhead
Scribbling on the sky the message He Is Dead,
Put crepe bows round the white necks of the public doves,
Let the traffic policemen wear black cotton gloves.

He was my North, my South, my East and West,
My working week and my Sunday rest,
My noon, my midnight, my talk, my song;
I thought that love would last forever: I was wrong.

The stars are not wanted now; put out every one:
Pack up the moon and dismantle the sun;
Pour away the ocean and sweep up the woods:
For nothing now can ever come to any good.

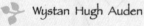 Wystan Hugh Auden

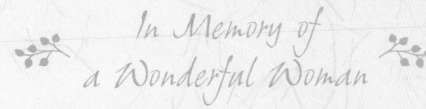

In Memory of
a Wonderful Woman

Woman much missed, how you call to me, call to me,
Saying that now you are not as you were
When you had changed from the one who was all to me,
But as at first, when our day was fair.

Can it be you that I hear? Let me view you, then,
Standing as when I drew near to the town
Where you would wait for me: yes, as I knew you then,
Even to the original air-blue gown!

Or is it only the breeze, in its listlessness
Travelling across the wet mead to me here,
You being ever dissolved to wan wistlessness,
Heard no more again far or near?

Thus I; faltering forward,
Leaves around me falling,
Wind oozing thin through the thorn from norward,
And the woman calling.

Thomas Hardy

Miss You

I miss you in the morning, dear,
  When all the world is new;
I know the day can bring no joy
  Because it brings not you.
I miss the well-loved voice of you,
  Your tender smile for me,
The charm of you, the joy of your
  Unfailing sympathy.

The world is full of folks, it's true,
  But there was only one of you.

I miss you at the noontide, dear;
  The crowded city street
Seems but a desert now, I walk
  In solitude complete.

I miss your hand beside my own
 The light touch of your hand,
The quick gleam in the eyes of you
 So sure to understand.

The world is full of folks, it's true,
 But there was only one of you.

I miss you in the evening, dear,
 When daylight fades away;
I miss the sheltering arms of you
 To rest me from the day,
I try to think I see you yet
 There where the firelight gleams —
Weary at last, I sleep, and still
 I miss you in my dreams.

The world is full of folks, it's true,
 But there was only one of you.

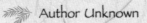 Author Unknown

Do not come when I am dead
To sit beside a low green mound,
Or bring the first gay daffodils
Because I love them so,
For I shall not be there.
You cannot find me there.

I will look up at you from the eyes
Of little children;
I will bend to meet you in the swaying boughs
Of bud-thrilled trees,
And caress you with the passionate sweep
Of storm-filled winds;
I will give you strength in your upward tread
Of everlasting hills;
I will cool your tired body in the flow
Of the limpid river;

I will warm your work-glorified hands through the glow
Of the winter fire;
I will soothe you into forgetfulness to the drop, drop
Of the rain on the roof;
I will speak to you out of the rhymes
Of the Masters;
I will dance with you in the lilt
Of the violin,
And make your heart leap with the bursting cadence
Of the organ;
I will flood your soul with the flaming radiance
Of the sunrise,
And bring you peace in the tender rose and gold
Of the after-sunset.

All these have made me happy:
They are a part of me;
I shall become a part of them.

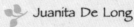 Juanita De Long

Know that there is no death, that all life is indivisible, that the here and hereafter are one, that time and eternity are inseparable, that this is one unobstructed universe. We are citizens of eternity.

Norman Vincent Peale

Their Works Follow Them

Blessed are the dead who die in the Lord. They rest from their labours — all their struggles, failures, past and over forever. But their works follow them. The good which they did on earth — that is not past and over. It cannot die. It lives and grows forever, following on in their path long after they are dead, and bearing fruit unto everlasting life, not only in them, but in men whom they never saw, and in generations yet unborn.

Charles Kingsley

We'll Understand

Not now, but in the coming years,
It may be in the Better Land,
We'll read the meaning of our tears,
And there, sometime, we'll understand.
We'll catch the broken threads again,
And finish what we here began;
Heaven will the mysteries explain,
And then, ah then, we'll understand.
We'll know why clouds instead of sun
Were over many a cherished plan;
Why sun has ceased, when scarce begun;
'Tis there, sometime, we'll understand.
God knows the way, He holds the key,
He guides us with unerring hand;
Sometimes with tearless eyes we'll see;
Yes, there, up there, we'll understand.
Then trust in God through all thy days;
Fear not, for he doth hold thy hand;
Though dark the way, still sing and praise;
Sometime, sometime, we'll understand.

Maxwell N. Cornelius

Remember

Remember me when I am gone away,
Gone far away into the silent land;
When you can no more hold me by the hand;
Nor I half turn to go, yet turning stay.
Remember me when no more, day by day,
You tell me of our future that you planned;
Only remember me; you understand
It will be late to counsel then or pray.

Yet if you should forget me for a while
And afterwards remember, do not grieve;
For if the darkness and corruption leave
A vestige of the thoughts that once I had,
Better by far you should forget and smile
Than that you should remember and be sad.

 Christina Rossetti

And there shall come a day... in Spring
When death and winter loose their chill, white hold
Quite suddenly. A day of sunlit air
When winging birds return,
And earth her gentle bosoms bare
So that new, thirsty life may nurture there.
That breathless hour...
So filled with warm, soft miracles
That faith is born anew.
On such a day... I shall return to you!
You may not touch me... no,
For you have thought of me as dead.
But in the silence lift believing eyes
Toward the dear infinity of skies. And listen...
With your very soul held still...
For you will hear me on some little hill,
Advancing with the coming of the year.
Not far away... Not dead... Not even gone.
The day will suddenly be filled
With immortality and song,
And without stirring from your quiet place,
Your love will welcome mine... across the little space,
And we will talk of every lovely thing...
When I return... in Spring!

Francesca Falk Miller

When I Am Gone

When I am gone release me
Let me go, I have so many things to see and do
You mustn't tie yourself to me with tears
Be happy that we had so many beautiful years
I gave to you my love
You can only guess how much you gave me in happiness
I thank you for the love you each have shown
But now it's time I travel alone
So grieve awhile for me, if grieve you must
Then let your grief be comforted by my trust
It's only for a while that we must part
So bless the memories within your heart
I won't be far away, for life goes on
So if you need me, call and I will come
Though you can't see or touch me, I'll be near
And if you listen within your heart you'll hear
All my love around you soft and clear
And then when you must come this way alone
I'll greet you with a smile and say
"Welcome Home."

Author Unknown

The loss of a person
is felt deeply by many
especially if that person
had a giving and touching life
I wish to express to you
my deepest sympathies
I will always remember
the life of
a very special person

Susan Polis Schutz

Were a star quenched on high,
For ages would its light,
Still travelling downward from the sky,
Shine on our mortal sight.
So when a great man dies,
For years beyond our ken,
The light he leaves behind him lies
Upon the paths of men.

Henry Wadsworth Longfellow

What we have done for ourselves alone dies with us; what we
have done for others and the world remains and is immortal.

Albert Pike

The Things That Never Die

The pure, the bright, the beautiful,
That stirred our hearts in youth,
The impulses to wordless prayer,
The dreams of love and truth;

The longings after something lost,
The spirit's yearning cry,
The strivings after better hopes —
These things can never die.

The timid hand stretched forth to aid
A brother in his need,
A kindly word in grief's dark hour
That proves a friend indeed;

The plea for mercy softly breathed,
When justice threatens nigh,
The sorrow of a contrite heart —
These things shall never die.

The cruel and bitter word,
That wounded as it fell;
The chilling want of sympathy
We feel, but never tell;
The hard repulse that chills the heart,
Whose hopes were bounding high,
In an unfading record kept —
These things shall never die.

Let nothing pass, for every hand
Must find some work to do;
Lose not a chance to waken love —

Be firm, and just, and true:
So shall a light that cannot fade
Beam on thee from on high,
And angel voices say to thee —
These things shall never die.

 — Charles Dickens

Those who have suffered much are like those who know many languages; they have learned to understand and to be understood by all.

Madame Swetchine

Time heals nothing — which should make us the better able to minister. There may be griefs beyond the reach of solace, but none worthy of the name that does not set free the springs of sympathy. Blessed are they that comfort, for they too have mourned, may be more likely the human truth.

Peter De Vries

Never does a man know the force that is in him until some mighty affection or grief has humanized the soul.

F. W. Robertson

To Those Who Weep

Your days must fill
With common tasks again; your path must go
Past where the springs of grief still overflow —
On bravely o'er the brow of Sorrow's hill;
For still there comes young laughter, and the call
Of life, that spurs to fresh endeavoring.
After the ice melts then the kind rains fall,
White trilliums bloom again in every spring.
So flowers of service blossom in us all —
The human heart is a courageous thing.

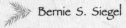 Anne Higginson Spicer

What can you do with sorrow and grief? You can accept them into your life the way water is accepted into the ground and taken up by the tree. Let these emotions become a part of your life without asking why. Accept life and death, experience the rituals of grief and sorrow, and free yourself to live. Grief and sorrow bring forth the tears that are the water the soul needs to survive. If you feel no sorrow and no grief, you will dry up and wither away as the tree does in a time of drought.

Bernie S. Siegel

A New Strength...

There are times in every life
when we feel hurt or alone...
But I believe that these times
when we feel lost
and all around us seems
     to be falling apart
    are really bridges of growth.
We struggle and try to recapture
    the security of what was,
     but almost in spite of ourselves
we emerge on the other side
with a new understanding,
    a new awareness,
    a new strength.
It is almost as though
    we must go through the pain
     and the struggle
      in order to grow
and reach new heights.

 Sue Mitchell

When you look up at the starlit sky
know that you are not alone
In your loss, you have gained a
guiding light, an angel by your side
You may feel lonely and hurt inside
as this moment overwhelms you
But time will bring you closer to
understanding, and it will slowly fill
the emptiness inside your heart
You have friends and family to help you
through this, but you have someone
even greater watching over you now
Let the sunlight dry the tears that flow
from your eyes, and as the sun sets
into night, know that you are not alone
Know that among the beauty of the night
a soul twinkles just for you
And that in the calmness of a passing breeze
peace floats by to ease your heart
As long as the day turns into night
you should never feel lonely
because you are not alone

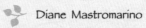 Diane Mastromarino

When a Blossom Falls

When a tree bursts forth into bloom,
we are drawn like magnets
to the brilliant array
of color and fragrance.
When we look closely, we see
that every individual blossom
contains its own pattern and beauty.
Each blossom has a purpose —
to resist the elements of time
and give support and life
to all the other blossoms.
When a blossom falls,
the physical form leaves us,
but the legacy lives on
in those it leaves behind.
Remember the softness,
the fragrance, vitality, and freshness...
remember all the beauty
when a blossom falls.

Geri Danks

Memories Keep Those We Love
Close to Us Forever

Although words seem to say so little,
may they help in some small way
to ease the sense of loss
that you're experiencing.
Hold fast to your memories,
to all the cherished moments of the past,
to the blessings and the laughter,
the joys and the celebrations,
the sorrow and the tears.
They all add up to a treasure
of fond yesterdays
that you shared and spent together,
and they keep the one you loved
close to you in spirit and thought.
The special moments
and memories in your life
will never change.
They will always be in your heart,
today and forevermore.

Linda E. Knight

ACKNOWLEDGMENTS

We gratefully acknowledge the permission granted by the following authors, publishers, and authors' representatives to reprint poems or excerpts from their publications.

Linda E. Knight for "To Everything, There Is a Season...." Copyright © 2000 by Linda E. Knight. All rights reserved.

Golden Quill Press for "Death Is a Door" by Nancy Byrd Turner. Copyright © by Golden Quill Press, Tucson, Arizona. All rights reserved.

Robert L. Bell for "Ships Returning Home" by Max Ehrmann. Copyright © 1948 by Bertha K. Ehrmann. All rights reserved. Reprinted by permission of Robert L. Bell, Melrose, MA 02176.

PrimaDonna Entertainment Corp. for "The Loss of a Loved One Is Never Easy" by Donna Fargo. Copyright © 2000 by PrimaDonna Entertainment Corp. All rights reserved.

Random House, Inc., for "No one can tell you..." from GRIEVING: A LOVE STORY by Ruth Coughlin. Copyright © 1993 by Ruth Coughlin. And for "Stop all the clocks..." from COLLECTED POEMS by W. H. Auden. Copyright © 1940, renewed 1968 by W. H. Auden. All rights reserved.

HarperCollins Publishers for "To One in Sorrow" from SONGS OF HOPE by Grace Noll Crowell. Copyright © 1939 by Harper & Brothers, renewed 1966 by Grace Noll Crowell. And for "Memory is more..." from THE SACRED JOURNEY by Frederick Buechner. Copyright © 1982 by Frederick Buechner. And for "What can you do..." from HOW TO LIVE BETWEEN OFFICE VISITS by Bernie S. Siegel, M.D. Copyright © 1993 by Bernie S. Siegel. All rights reserved.

Perseus Books for "I didn't plan..." from MOTHERLESS DAUGHTERS by Hope Edelman. Copyright © 1995 by Hope Edelman. All rights reserved.

Dr. Joy Browne for "There's a prayer..." from NOBODY'S PERFECT: ADVICE FOR BLAME-FREE LIVING, published by Simon & Schuster. Copyright © 1988 by Dr. Joy Browne. All rights reserved.

Alfred A. Knopf, Inc., a division of Random House, Inc., and the Gibran National Committee, Beirut, Lebanon, for "You would know..." from THE PROPHET by Kahlil Gibran. Copyright © 1923 by Kahlil Gibran and renewed 1951 by Administrators C.T.A. of Kahlil Gibran Estate and Mary G. Gibran. All rights reserved.

Regnery Publishing, Inc., for "Departed Friends" from COLLECTED VERSE OF EDGAR GUEST. Copyright © 1934 by Henry Regnery Publishing. All rights reserved. Reprinted by special permission of Regnery Publishing, Inc., Washington, D.C.

Simon & Schuster for "Know that there is no death..." from POSITIVE THINKING EVERY DAY by Norman Vincent Peale. Copyright © 1993 by Dr. Norman Vincent Peale. All rights reserved.

The Estate of Peter De Vries for "Time heals nothing..." from THE BLOOD OF THE LAMB by Peter De Vries, published by Little, Brown and Company. Copyright © 1961 by Peter De Vries. All rights reserved.

Sue Mitchell for "A New Strength...." Copyright © 1981 by Sue Mitchell. All rights reserved.

Diane Mastromarino for "When you look up at the starlit sky...." Copyright © 2000 by Diane Mastromarino. All rights reserved.

Geri Danks for "When a Blossom Falls." Copyright © 2000 by Geri Danks. All rights reserved.

A careful effort has been made to trace the ownership of poems used in this anthology in order to obtain permission to reprint copyrighted materials and give proper credit to the copyright owners. If any error or omission has occurred, it is completely inadvertent, and we would like to make corrections in future editions provided that written notification is made to the publisher.

SPS STUDIOS, INC., P.O. Box 4549, Boulder, Colorado 80306.

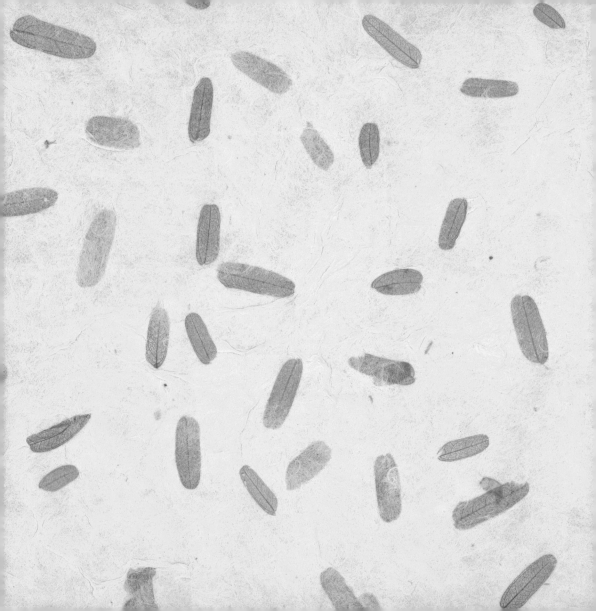

You would know the secret of death.

But how shall you find it unless you seek it in the heart of life?

The owl whose night-bound eyes are blind unto the day cannot unveil the mystery of light.

If you would indeed behold the spirit of death, open your heart wide unto the body of life.

For life and death are one, even as the river and the sea are one.

In the depth of your hopes and desires lies your silent knowledge of the beyond;

And like seeds dreaming beneath the snow your heart dreams of spring.

Trust the dreams, for in them is hidden the gate to eternity.

Your fear of death is but the trembling of the shepherd when he stands before the king whose hand is to be laid upon him in honour.

Consolation Is...

...like a seed that lies planted in the soul. It cannot and it will not bloom in the winter of the heart's grief, for winter is not its season. Instead, it lies dormant — for years, sometimes — until sorrow washes away, bright and clear, and leaves a space for consolation to grow. In that moment, it draws from the long roots it has been growing in the heart and blossoms forth in clusters of beautiful memories.

Jordan St. Cyr

...the great gift that is yours to share with another soul in sorrow. It can be expressed best not in words, but simply by your silent presence and your willingness to stand beside this person as they seek a way through the vast and personal labyrinth of mourning.

Lawrence B. Tavernas

...a little like a journey that each man must find his own map to navigate by.

Jon Ericksson